THE SECRETS OF
SCOTLAND

METRO BOOKS
New York

An Imprint of Sterling Publishing
387 Park Avenue South
New York, NY 10016

Publisher and Creative Director: Nick Wells
Project Editor: Esme Chapman
Art Director: Mike Spender
Layout Design: Mike Spender
Digital Design and Production: Chris Herbert

Thanks to: Frances Bodiam, Sarah Goulding, Sara Robson, Melinda Révész, Claire Walker, Polly Willis.

All photographs in this book by Dennis Hardley
www.scotphoto.com

Dennis Hardley (photographs) was born in Blitz-sieged Liverpool in 1940, where he spent his teenage years doing
odd jobs for the Beatles before becoming a Concorde engineer. Dennis first became a photographer as an RAF civilian
in 1972, supplying pictures to *Scots Magazine*. In 1973, he moved to Scotland with his family and established himself as a
professional photographer. He has since driven over a million miles in his pursuit of photographing the Scottish landscape,
and this is the fifth book to feature his work.

Dedication: I would like to thank my wife Dorothy for her continuing support, my son Tony who runs the business with me,
and Fiona Elise, our live-in granddaughter whose vibrant personality has brought so much pleasure to our lives. I would like
to dedicate this book to my father, Harold Hardley, aged 91. A wonderful human being.

Michael Kerrigan (text) lives in Edinburgh, where he writes regularly for the *Scotsman* newspaper. He is a book reviewer for
the *Times Literary Supplement* and the *Guardian*, London. As an author, he has published extensively on both British and world
history and prehistory. He has been a contributor to Flame Tree's *World History* and *Irish History* as well as to the *Times Encyclopaedia
of World Religion* (2001). He is currently working on an account of Charles Darwin and the voyage of the Beagle.

ISBN 978-1-4351-5550-3

For information about custom editions, special sales, and premium and corporate purchases,
please contact Sterling Special Sales at 800–805–5489 or specialsales@sterlingpublishing.com

Manufactured in China

1 3 5 7 9 10 8 6 4 2

www.sterlingpublishing.com

THE SECRETS OF
SCOTLAND

PHOTOGRAPHS BY DENNIS HARDLEY
Text by Michael Kerrigan

METRO BOOKS
New York

CONTENTS

CONTENTS

INTRODUCTION

"When I am asked about Scotland how did I like it, my enthusiasm for it makes people repent of their question and I must remember that I am in England which is jealous of the land of the mountain and the flood."

Krystyn Lach-Syrma spent over three years in Scotland, from 1820, with the two Polish princes to whom he was tutor. The country was enjoying something of a 'Golden Age' just then: the visitor met Sir Walter Scott, James Hogg and other luminaries – his royal pupils were a passport to the most fashionable soirées and the stateliest homes. In 1824, he headed south with his young charges for a season in London, but his letter to a friend in Scotland makes clear just how profound an impression the country had made on him. Was the remark about English "jealousy" justified? We can only wonder: what *is* clear is how strong a proxy-patriot he had become. He was not the first foreign visitor to fall in love with Scotland, of course; he would certainly not be the last.

Where he differs from many more recent visitors, however, is in the breadth of his affections: it was as much as anything the variety of the Scottish scene that stirred his soul. *From Charlotte Square to Fingal's Cave* (tr. Helena Brochowska, ed. Mona McLeod, 2004) is the memoir of the time he spent in Scotland. Intelligent and insightful as it frequently is, what is striking to the reader today is his receptiveness to the variety of what the country had to offer. Though Scotland was to him (in Burns's phrase) "the land of the mountain and the flood", it was also the land of the factory and the canal. He was as susceptible as any romantic visitor to the grandeur of a Highland glen, but he could appreciate a classical façade or ornamental shrubbery too. He thrilled to hear tales of kilted cattle-raiders but admired the industry and ingenuity of the Lowland farmer, and revered the scholars of Scotland's medieval universities. He loved the writings of Walter Scott, but was every bit as excited at the cutting-edge researches of Scottish scientists and the new industries which technology had opened the way to.

It is in just this spirit that this book sets out to reveal *The Secrets of Scotland* – the full diversity of the Scottish scene is presented here. Dennis Hardley has explored the remotest reaches of the Highlands and Islands to find vistas of heartstopping sublimity and haunting atmosphere. A lyrical poet with the camera, he reminds us once again of the exhilarating beauty of a country whose wild ruggedness has caught the imagination of the world. But he captures another country, too: some of the best-kept secrets, famously, are hidden in open view, and Hardley finds fresh inspiration in less obviously dramatic settings. Here are winding rivers, rolling fields, orderly parklands, neat little textile towns and magnificent mansions – not to mention the busy streets and squares of modern cities.

For the sake of convenience and clarity, this book divides the country into separate regions. Necessarily, these divisions are – to some degree – arbitrary. Yet there are clear distinctions between the different parts of Scotland – not only in geology, landscape and geographical situation, but in their often vastly dissimilar experiences over several thousand years. The Western Isles, which for several centuries history tied more closely to Scandinavia than to Scotland, have developed a special character all their own. As time went on a Gaelic tradition would emerge, linking Lewis, Harris and the other outer Isles more closely with the Northern Highlands: the counties of Caithness, Sutherland, Ross and Cromarty, the region we move on to consider next. The Southern Highlands, as covered here, embraces the area to the south of

Inverness and includes Strathspey and Nairn as well as Lochaber and Lochalsh. In geological and scenic terms, the Inner Hebrides (Skye, Mull, Islay, Colonsay and many more) can be seen as continuations of the Southern Highlands, but their history – and of course their island culture – sets them apart. To the east of the Highlands proper sprawl the Grampians, just as mountainous at their centre but sloping down to the gentler country of the coast. Tucked-away fishing villages line the North Sea shoreline –

Around the Firth of Forth is to be found the heart of historic Scotland: the cathedral and castle at St Andrews, the palace at Linlithgow and, of course, Edinburgh. Yet history plays strange tricks: through much of the first millennium AD, the Lothians formed part of the Anglo-Saxon kingdom of Northumbria. Edinburgh, a Celtic hillfort, was a hotly contested site. Pulled back and forth between Picts and Angles, it finally fell to the former, but Scotland's future capital had come within a whisker of being an 'English' city. Not that Scotland as we know it existed yet: much of the next region, the area now covered by Glasgow, the Clyde Valley and Argyll, belonged (with the inshore islands) to the Celtic kingdom of Dál Riata. This was essentially an Irish realm, the Glens of Antrim its originating centre; the North Channel functioned not as a frontier but as a connecting link. It may seem strange from a modern standpoint, but with such difficult terrain to the landward side, this part of Scotland naturally looked westward out to sea.

It just goes to show how misleading simplistic notions of 'Scottishness' may be, a fact only underlined when we come to consider the southwest. Just across the border from England lies one of Scotland's least-known regions, a place apart even in the Scottish scheme of things. From its wild hills to its isolated farmsteads, Galloway gives the impression of being out on a geographical and cultural limb; even Ayrshire feels aloof from the country as a whole. To the east, Dumfries gives on to the contested territory of the Borders, a region formed by several centuries of incessant conflict. Its identity ambivalent, it defined itself against the England with which its inhabitants were so much of the time at war – but in doing so it set itself apart to a certain extent from the rest of Scotland.

largely unknown to the outsider; here too is the 'Granite City', Aberdeen. There are more cities to the south in central Scotland, notably Dundee, Perth and Stirling – but also some of the country's most spectacular scenes. The 'Lowlands' begin here, but as this and succeeding chapters show, landscapes in this region are often hilly by any normal standards.

In the end, though, it has to be faced that if there is one single thing that binds Scotland together as a nation, it is the age-old rivalry – long an actual enmity – with England. That is clear in what is widely seen as the country's founding document, the Declaration of Arbroath, which was signed by the Scottish lords in 1320. If Robert the Bruce sold Scotland out to England, they warned,

"… we should exert ourselves at once to drive him out as our enemy and a subverter of his own rights and ours, and make some other man who was well able to defend us our King; for, as long as but a hundred of us remain alive, never will we on any conditions be brought under English rule."

Brave words, which many Scots felt had to be eaten after the Union of the Parliaments in 1707, though this would, in theory, be a marriage of equal partners rather than an act of domination. Though staged specifically in support of the claims of the House of Stewart to rule in Britain as a whole, the Jacobite rebellions of 1715 and 1745 have often been seen as being broadly nationalistic in their inspiration. But Scottish opinion was bitterly divided on these uprisings, and Scots made up the bulk of the armies that quelled them: many were strongly in favour of the Union.

In part this was because Presbyterian Scots felt more in common with a Protestant England than they did with the Catholic-leaning Stewarts and their continental allies. Scots 'Covenanters' in the seventeenth century had rebelled against Stewart England on religious grounds; now the same loyalties drew many to set aside the national enmities of old. The Reformation made its unmistakeable mark on Scotland: Protestantism would prove an important aspect of the identity of the modern Scot, who was stereotypically dour. Even here, though, it is dangerous to generalize: parts of the Highlands and Islands remained resolutely Catholic, whilst the nineteenth century saw Catholic immigrants streaming in from famine-stricken Ireland to the Lowland cities.

Subsequent waves of immigration from southern and eastern Europe, the Indian subcontinent and other parts of the world have seen the emergence of a modern multicultural society in Scotland. As elsewhere, that has not been without its challenges. Historically, however, Scotland has been a country in which different cultures, apparently ill-suited, have been able to come together in a common patriotic cause.

WESTERN ISLES

The Western Isles are a place apart, not so much the Outer Hebrides as the Outer Darkness as far as generations of English – and even Scots – have been concerned.

That alien quality is by no means entirely imaginary – these islands were ruled by the Kings of Norway until well into the thirteenth century and, since then, the Gaelic tongue has been spoken here. Yet the 'Long Island' of Lewis and Harris and its southward-straggling tail of smaller islands (North Uist, Benbecula, South Uist, Barra and Mingulay) can claim to be the oldest region of the British Isles. Britain's most ancient rock strata are found here, formed some 2,700 million years ago, along with some of the earliest signs of human settlement, from around 4000 BC. Today, scattered ruins remain – in particular those standing stones which, though clear signs of human presence, merely underline the eerie emptiness of the Hebridean landscape.

Lashed by Atlantic storms for much of the year, far removed from centres of modernity, the Outer Hebrides have a distinctly forgotten feel. But by the same token they are utterly unspoiled; their beauty, though sometimes austere, is often breathtaking, and when the sun comes out there is no more exquisite spot on earth.

HARBOUR AND TOWN
Stornoway, Isle of Lewis

A Mediterranean sun lights up Stornoway and its lovely natural harbour, belying the Western Isles' reputation for barrenness. "On the contrary," wrote Dean Monro, a cleric who came here in 1549, Lewis was "fair and well inhabited at the coast, fertile and fruitful." The Outer Hebrides' only significant town, Stornoway has weathered economic turbulence of late, with downturns in tweedmaking and the vital herring fishery. But these blows have been cushioned by the rise of the tourist industry: Stornoway today is a thriving regional capital.

CROFT
Baleshare, North Uist

In the rose-tinted twilight of summer, a croft seems an inseparable feature of the landscape, the mass of Ben Eaval rising in the rear. An idyllic scene, it gives no clue to the backbreaking labour required to work the unyielding soils of the island interiors, or the dangers faced by generations of crofters when they set to sea to supplement their food supply by fishing. Today, a dying tradition may have found a new lease of life thanks to mounting interest in cultural continuity and agricultural sustainability.

CROFTS AT CARINISH
Ardnastruban, North Uist

So much sky, sea and silver sand and so little human habitation: nothing can prepare the visitor for the far-flung openness of the Hebridean landscape. Here, looking west to the crofts of Carinish from the causeway linking North Uist with Benbecula, there is a heartstopping sense of space, fresh air and freedom. Little more than a stepping stone between the two Uists, Benbecula is often passed through without pause on the north–south journey – a pity, as it is a place of unforgettable beauty.

FOLLY
Loch Scalpaig, North Uist

Standing on an islet with the loch for a moat, this little castle is no more than a modern folly, but the warlike past it evokes was real enough. First assaulted by Viking raids, the Western Isles were eventually absorbed into Norwegian territory, before being ruled – as a separate realm – by the 'Lords of the Isles'. Not until 1493 were they finally brought under Scottish rule after a bitter struggle, and there were sporadic rebellions against the Crown for several generations.

STONE CIRCLE
Callanish, Isle of Lewis

A visit to the stone circle at Callanish is a truly unforgettable experience: stand here and look, and feel the millennia melt away. Babylon was not built when ancient masons started raising these megaliths 5,000 years ago, but this gusty promontory above Loch Roag probably looked much the same as it does now. Much is still to be discovered about the lives of Lewis's first human inhabitants, but there is widespread evidence of settlement dating back to the earliest Neolithic times.

TOWARDS THE NORTH HARRIS HILLS
Luskentyre, South Harris

The afterglow of a smouldering sundown sets sea and sky
ablaze, a dramatic frame for this splendid view of the North
Harris hills. In the foreground, waves wash the mudflats just
offshore at Luskentyre; beyond lie the deeper waters of the
Sound of Taransay. It is a ravishing sight and, in this modern
age, an exceptional one: no man-made interference disrupts
the symphonic play of natural light. No sodium streetlamp
glare, no headlights, no shop signs are to be seen; not even
the merest glint from a cottage window.

ST CLEMENT'S CHURCH
Rodel, South Harris

There is believed to have been a church at Rodel for
several centuries. Visiting Harris in 1549, Dean Monro noted
"a monastery with a steeple". The structure he saw is thought
to have been newly built – though completed just in time,
as it turned out – to have its function abolished by the
Scottish Reformation. Far removed from ecclesiastical oversight,
Catholicism clung on in a number of the Western Isles, but
those that converted (including Harris) adopted an especially
ferocious form of Protestantism.

M.V. CLANSMAN
Castlebay, Isle of Barra

The M.V. *Clansman* takes centre stage in this view of Castlebay Harbour, Barra, and rightly so: the 'Cal Mac' (Caledonian MacBrayne) ferries are the mainstay of island life. Carrying passengers, post, cars and freight of every kind, they ply back and forth daily linking 22 different Hebridean isles in total, and provide an essential connection with the mainland. On the hillside above the harbour stands the Church of Our Lady, Star of the Sea. Barra is one of those islands whose people remained Catholic despite the Reformation.

LEVERBURGH
South Harris

As recently as 1921 this little township in southern Harris was known as Obbe: it was renamed in honour of Lord Leverhulme, who had bought both Lewis and Harris. The wealthy manufacturer of Sunlight Soap was also a dreamer-up of ambitious social schemes – he planned to make this the productive centre serving his nationwide fishmongers' chain 'MacFisheries'. Like so many before him, Leverhulme ran up against the islanders' independent spirit. He gave up and moved on, his only legacy his name.

TRAIGH MHOR BEACH
Isle of Barra

Traigh Mhor Beach on the northeastern side of Barra has for centuries been celebrated for its cockles; more recently it has doubled as a landing strip. The famous writer, Compton Mackenzie, built a bungalow above this beach in 1934, where he wrote many of his most famous works including the classic comic novel *Whisky Galore* (1947). He based his story on an actual incident, the foundering of the whisky-laden SS *Politician*, which was wrecked at Calvay, just off the neighbouring island of Eriksay, in 1941.

HARBOUR
Kallin, Isle of Grimsay

Grimsay lies between Benbecula and North Uist, and until recently it was almost impossible to reach. Surrounded at high tide by waters too shallow for navigation, at low water by sands too soft for safe passage, it was isolated even by island standards. Now a causeway links it to its neighbours, and Grimsay's prosperity has soared. The harbour at Kallin was built as recently as 1985, and the trade in specialised seafood for continental markets and the advent of fish farming have held out new economic hope for the Hebrides.

NORTHERN HIGHLANDS

There are parts of the northern Highlands where you can walk all day without finding a road; before the eighteenth century you could have gone a week or more.

That was when General Wade set about building his network of military roads – part of the pacification programme for a seditious and unruly region. Here, the House of Hanover knew, the people's first loyalty lay not with their official monarchy but with their clan chieftains; their second, often as not, with the Stewarts 'across the water'.

Today the tumults are long gone, though there is a melancholy edge to the prevailing peace and quiet. As elsewhere in the Highlands, the 'unspoiled' character is not entirely natural. Shamefully sold out by their chiefs, thousands of the rural poor were forced off their smallholdings in the 'Clearances' of the nineteenth century to make way for more lucrative sheep-farming.

Oddly, the northernmost part of the region, Caithness, is the gentlest when it comes to scenery, its green fields contrasting starkly with Sutherland's wild mountains and desolate moors. Wester Ross has some of Scotland's most stunning upland views, and the entire northwest coast is one of the scenic wonders of the British Isles.

EILEAN DONAN CASTLE
Loch Duich, Ross-shire

The castle was rebuilt in the early twentieth century, with scant regard for historical accuracy, but Scotland's most photographed fortress is no mere folly. In fact, its story is as romantic as its setting. Built in the fourteenth century (the surrounding wall is even older), the family seat of the Mackenzies became one of the bases for the Jacobite rising of 1719. A Spanish garrison sat helplessly here whilst the warships of the Crown reduced the walls to rubble all around them.

HELMSDALE HARBOUR
Caithness

"It has an excellent harbour," wrote Robert Chambers in the 1820s, "to which immense armadas of fishing boats resort during the herring season." A Lowlander, Chambers had no reason to consider the cost of this prosperity in human terms. The fishing port had been established by the Duke of Sutherland in 1818, as part of a wider scheme of economic redevelopment involving the expulsion of over 15,000 tenants from his lands. A few found employment here: the rest were forced to emigrate to North America, Australia and New Zealand.

STAC POLLY
Inverpolly, Sutherland

Occasionally picturesque, the Northern Highlands are often awesomely spectacular, but sometimes they are eerily primeval in their beauty. Here Stac Polly rises high above the placid waters of Loch Lurgain in a scene that cannot have changed much over several million years. Up close, Stac Polly looks very different, countless centuries of wind and weather having eroded its soft sandstone into myriad exotic forms. It has become an adventure playground for climbers, who congregate here each weekend to explore its jagged outcrops and tackle its dizzying pinnacles.

RIVER LAXFORD AND BEN ARKLE
Sutherland

It looks like a dusting of snow, but it is actually the quartzite crystal from which Ben Arkle is largely formed that makes the mountain sparkle so in the summer sunshine. In the foreground, the River Laxford winds lazily through one of northwest Sutherland's remotest 'straths' (broad valleys). *Laks* is the old Germanic word for 'salmon' (hence the Swedish *gravadlax* or the Yiddish *lox* and bagels), and is the reason why the Vikings so-named a river which even today has some of Scotland's most sought-after (and expensive!) salmon fishing.

LOCHINVER
Sutherland

This tiny west Sutherland settlement had its heyday in the 1880s when this "beautiful rising watering-place" boasted two hotels. Genteel holidaymakers were drawn here by the prospect of plentiful fresh air and fishing, while regular steamers offered a connection down the coast to Oban. Today, while tourism remains significant, as it does throughout the Highland region, commercial fishing and fish-farming have overtaken it in importance. Fortunately, Lochinver and its environs have remained substantially unspoiled, as this view across the town to the peak of Suilven clearly shows.

PORT OF ULLAPOOL
Wester Ross

Ullapool occupies the only significant stretch of level ground
to be found around the rugged shores of Loch Broom in
Wester Ross, with its name believed to have derived from its
foundation by a Norseman named 'Olaf'. The railway never
quite made it here, despite the passing of an Act of Parliament
(1890) authorising construction, but this has remained the
major port for ferries to the outer isles. It is now a major
tourist centre, the perfect holiday base for anybody wishing
to explore the northern Highlands.

BERRIEDALE
Caithness

In its recent rage for economic diversification, this Caithness
village has embraced everything from bottled water to llama
farming, but its pathways still seem to lead naturally to the sea.
Its single street stands just above the shoreline in a secluded and
sheltered inlet of one of Scotland's most rugged and storm-swept
coasts, the perfect site for what was always first and foremost a
fishing centre. Down a beautiful valley above the village runs a
river, Berriedale Water, undoubtedly one of Scotland's best-kept
scenic secrets.

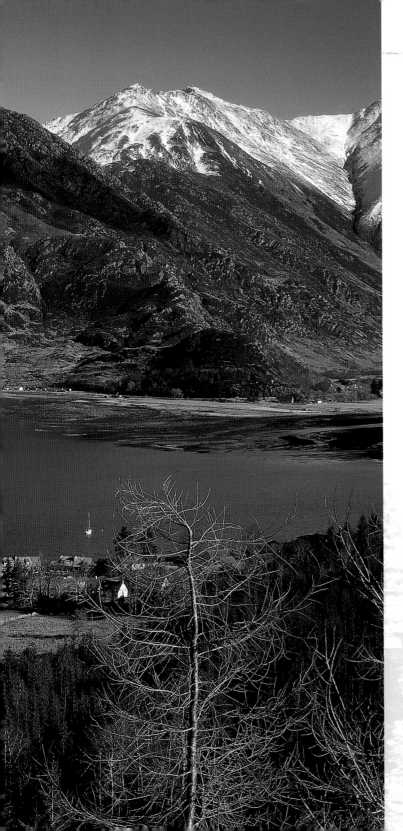

MAM RATAGAN PASS
Ross-shire

Mam Ratagan was once the main route across the western hills for drovers herding livestock to the markets of the Lowlands. The scenery is stunning, but it is safe to assume this was wasted on cattle thoroughly traumatized after the enforced swim over the sea from Skye. Today's tourist can, however, appreciate the view across Loch Duich to the peaks of Kintail, said to have been five forsaken brides – a local chieftain's daughters – turned to stone out of pity by a sorcerer's spell.

LOCH MAREE
Wester Ross

A solitary pine stands sentinel by a snaking road above the waters of Loch Maree in Wester Ross, with Ben Slioch rising in the distance and clouds that seem to curdle an ethereal azure sky. The whole scene might have been dreamed into existence as a landscape fit for a mythical hero to make his way across en route to some fateful encounter with his destiny. The Highland terrain itself is acknowledged to offer some of the finest scenery in the world: add in the Highland light and we have something almost spectral, otherworldly.

KEISS CASTLE
Sutherland

Majestic even in its ruined state – perhaps still more dramatic that way – Keiss Castle stands sublime atop a rocky outcrop above Sinclair's Bay. George Sinclair, Fifth Earl of Caithness, was the warlord who built this imposing stronghold for himself in the late sixteenth century – though it had fallen into dereliction by 1700. South of here, Caithness's eastern coast starts to become noticeably gentler in character, in contrast with the rocky cliffs and promontories to be seen around the shoreline to the north.

FALLS OF ROGIE
Easter Ross

Deep in the Torrachilty Forest, a couple of miles to the west of Contin, Easter Ross, the Black Water River thunders over the Falls of Rogie. Although a splendid sight for the spellbound visitor, it represents a serious obstacle for the salmon which have to make their way upstream to reach their ancestral spawning grounds each year. Remarkably, many succeed in making the leap – an extraordinary feat of animal athleticism. For those who fail, a salmon ladder has now been built alongside the waterfall.

DUNROBIN CASTLE
Golspie, Caithness

Dunrobin Castle is more a château than a castle in the conventional sense. It was actually built around a genuine medieval core, laid down in 1275 by Robert, Earl of Sutherland, on a strategic sea-coast site north of Golspie in Caithness. No sign of that can be seen in the structure as re-imagined in the 1840s by Sir Charles Barry, architect of the Palace of Westminster, however. An extravagant Gothic confection, with spacious ornamental grounds extending landward, it was conceived with gracious living rather than defence in mind.

SINCLAIR AND GIRNIGOE CASTLE
Wick, Caithness

Another stronghold of the Sinclair family, this twofold
fortress stands on Noss Head, just north of Wick, Caithness;
Girnigoe Castle, the original structure, dates from around
1480. The more elegant and commodious Sinclair Castle was
built a little way inland in 1606. Since this contained the
family's living quarters, it bore the brunt of the cannonade
when the Clan Campbell came calling in 1690. It is ironic,
then, that the medieval section is in better repair than its
more modern counterpart, but an ambitious scheme is under
way with hopes of restoring both.

SOUTHERN HIGHLANDS

From Nairn, south through Strathspey and Lochaber, lies some of Scotland's most spectacular scenery, and westward across the Great Glen is even more.

Ben Nevis, Britain's highest peak, is here, though at only 1,344 m (4,408 ft) it would scarcely qualify as a hill in any of the truly mountainous regions of the world. But then that is arguably what makes the Scottish Highlands so special: they offer sublimity on a human scale.

A sense of human history always haunts the visitor here. Every mountain, every glen, every pass has its own story. Old battlefields; ruined castles; the abandoned cottages of the Clearances: the memories of past tragedies are a living presence in the landscape. A stunning setting by any standards, Glencoe undoubtedly has an extra resonance thanks to a consciousness of the terrible deeds done here three centuries ago. The Highland scene is not merely beautiful but romantic, a stage on which great and terrible dramas have been enacted.

Yet, if the melancholy minor key is always present, it is hard to stay sombre for long: the loveliness of the landscape is exhilarating. A burst of sunshine, a new vista — wherever one goes, there is something fresh and delightful to be seen.

GREIG STREET BRIDGE

Inverness

The Greig Street suspension bridge spans the fast-flowing River Ness, and was completed in 1881. The great German novelist Theodor Fontane observed when he visited the town in the 1850s that Inverness always was "a forward-thrusting town". Though often patronized by outsiders, who assume it to be a sleepy backwater, the 'capital of the Highlands' has always been remarkable for its liveliness and energy. Since the millennium it has been – by royal appointment – not a town but a city, looking forward optimistically to the future .

HIGHLAND COW

Western Highlands

She may look a little grotesque beside the sleeker breeds that one is used to seeing, but the Highland cow is perfectly adapted to her Highland setting. Far from impeding vision, the long fringe helps protect the eyes from flies and parasites and the shaggy coat keeps out the searing cold, the biting winds and squalls of snow and rain. Despite her impressive horns she has an exceptionally placid disposition, while her stocky build gives her toughness: Highland cattle are strongly resistant to disease. Low birth-weight makes calving less complicated and more safe.

URQUHART CASTLE
Loch Ness, Inverness-shire

On a little promontory of land jutting out into Loch Ness
stands the ancient fortress known as Urquhart Castle. There
was a fort here in the Iron Age; the first 'modern' castle dates
from the twelfth century but it has been razed and rebuilt
several times in the centuries since. England's Edward I,
'Hammer of the Scots', seized it in 1296 and again in 1308 –
Robert I of Scotland retook it that same year. It went on to
feature in the rebellions of both the Covenanters and Jacobites.

GLEN NEVIS
Lochaber

Sunshine and fresh snow, a ravishing combination in any
Highland setting, lends a wonderful jewelled beauty to this
Lochaber scene. To the right, the Water of Nevis flows on
unfrozen, its clear stream an impenetrable black against its
dazzling background; beyond spreads the exquisite tracery
of the trees. A deep, steep-sided valley gouged out by glaciers
in successive ice ages, Glen Nevis skirts the southwestern
edge of the Ben Nevis range. Britain's highest summit is covered
with snow for much of the year.

THE PRINCE'S MONUMENT
Loch Shiel, Glenfinnan

On this patch of boggy ground beside Loch Shiel, the standard
of the Jacobites was raised at the start of the great rebellion of
1745. Taken from *Jacobus*, the Latin for James, the Jacobites
supported the claim to the crown of James VII of the House
of Stewart, now passed to his son, the 'Young Pretender',
Bonnie Prince Charlie. The rebels had some success at first,
getting as far south as Derby in their march on London, before
being turned back and finally defeated at Culloden.

LOCH QUOICH
Knoydart

If Knoydart is unspoiled, that is because it is almost impossible
to get to: this peninsula might just as well be an island. The walk
is long and difficult and the easiest way to reach it is by boat. Its
history is a dismal one, with its people being packed off to
Nova Scotia during the Clearances, but its beauty is enchanting
for all its desolation. Here we look westward through pine trees
across the waters of Loch Quoich, burnished by the blazing
splendour of a Knoydart sunset.

GLENFINNAN KIRK
Inverness-shire

Spring explodes in the Highlands like a sigh of relief after the
long, dark months of winter. Green leaves break forth, flowers
burst into bloom and cotton-wool clouds scud across the sky, as
though nature is trying its best to make up for lost time. St
Mary and St Finnan's Catholic Church, Glenfinnan, is perfectly
placed to enjoy the show, with stupendous views across Loch
Shiel. St Finnan, an early Irish missionary, is said to have had a
hermit's cell on an island in the loch.

GLENCOE

Inverness-shire

A hiker takes time out amidst the splendours of Glencoe.
The southern Highlands are perfectly suited to hill-walking
and climbing. Every grade of walk is to be had, from
decorous stroll to serious mountaineering – many routes,
of course, change their character with the season. Winter
walking is a specialized pursuit, to be undertaken only by
the experienced, and even then with careful preparation.
Even in summer, the Highlands must be treated with respect:
sudden storms may blow up out of nowhere, and
disorientating mists can descend when least expected.

FORT WILLIAM AND LOCH LINNHE
Inverness-shire

General Monck of Cromwell's Commonwealth army built a fort near here in 1654 as part of his wider plan to bring an unco-operative Scotland under control. It was rebuilt, reinforced and re-christened 'Fort William' in 1690, when the unseating of the Stewarts had set the Highlands seething. One of the biggest of the sea lochs, Loch Linnhe was not formed by glacial action like most of the others, but marks the southern end of that great geological fault which cleaves the Highlands down the middle.

RUTHVEN BARRACKS
Kingussie, Strathspey

The notorious fourteenth-century warlord, the Wolf of Badenoch, had his stronghold on this rise which controls comings and goings along the vital valley of Strathspey. After the Jacobite rising of 1715, Crown forces built a barracks, only to have it seized by the rebels in the course of the ''45'. The Jacobite survivors of Culloden holed up here to lick their wounds, and before dispersing, they blew it up to keep it out of government hands. So it still stands, a broken monument to shattered hopes and dreams.

TOWARDS EIGG AND RHUM
Glenuig Bay, Moidart

Looking out across a sparkling sea to the islands of Eigg and
Rhum, it is easy to see how the sea was for centuries seen as a
link and not a barrier. Given the difficulty of the terrain
ashore, it was often easier to travel by boat than it was by land,
except in the worst weather. For much of medieval history,
Moidart and the region around it were part of the territory of
the Lords of the Isles, looking west to the Hebrides, not
eastward to the rest of Scotland.

RANNOCH MOOR
Rannoch

"Here the crow starves," wrote T.S. Eliot, "…here the patient stag / Breeds for the rifle. Between the soft moor / And the soft sky, scarcely room / To leap or soar." There is an eerie otherworldliness about Rannoch even in the sunniest summer weather; in deep winter there is no bleaker place on earth.

CORPACH BASIN
Lochaber

Corpach marks the western end of the Great Glen, and the entrance to the Caledonian Canal which runs through the heart of the Highlands to emerge into the Moray Firth outside Inverness. Famous as the father of the steam engine, James Watt originally surveyed the course for this waterway, with construction undertaken by another distiguished engineer, Thomas Telford. But, heroic as their achievements were, they are dwarfed by those of nature, as exemplified by the brooding mass of Ben Nevis beyond Loch Linnhe.

SHEEP ON THE ROAD
Western Highlands

Through much of the British Isles these days, driving has become more vexation than pleasure. The Highlands are one of the few places where you can still find the 'open road', but if many of the cares of urban life may be forgotten here, traffic congestion can come in unexpected forms. On the narrow, single-track roads which predominate here, sheep may create their own little local rush-hours; the only thing the motorist can do in such a situation is to wait patiently.

LOCH LEVEN
Inverness-shire

Loch Leven is the looking-glass for this extraordinary image, its still waters reflecting the Mamore Hills and Glencoe village. A study in symmetry, it captures all the peace and tranquillity of a winter's day in which no sound breaks the silence, no ripple interrupts the water's surface. A branch of Loch Linnhe, narrow at the mouth, and crowded round by mountains on every side, Loch Leven is sheltered from the worst of the weather, its waters always comparatively calm.

INNER ISLANDS

"Well, here we are in Skye, and it feels like the South Seas" wrote the English novelist Virginia Woolf to her sister in 1938. It was not just the fact of being surrounded by sea, or her sense of remoteness from the railways and the London papers, but the almost mystic atmosphere, the eerie translucence of the air. "Hardly embodied," she elaborated, in a postcard to a friend: "Like living in a jellyfish lit up with green light."

Countless other visitors to the Inner Hebrides have experienced the same sense of strangeness, that trick of the light which lends a special resonance to every scene. Many seasoned Hebridean travellers insist that the Hebridean light varies considerably from isle to isle: Mull and Islay, they say, differ as much as Colonsay does from Kerrera. Others point more sceptically to the enormous variety of the islands in geological origins, landscape and history – naturally, each one has a different 'feel'.

What can hardly be disputed is the extraordinary beauty of the Inner Hebrides, and the remarkable variety of scenery they present. There are scores of islands here, each with its own distinctive character. You could explore them for years without ever exhausting their variety.

STORR ROCK
Trotternish, Isle of Skye

The tallest of these basalt pinnacles is known as 'the Old Man of Storr', which despite looking like a man-made megalith was formed naturally. Countless millennia of wind and rain wore away the softer rock around it, while other formations, every bit as strange, lie all around. Just across the Trotternish peninsula to westward, on the shores of Loch Kensaleyre, is a cluster of stones that really does seem to have been erected by humans. Legend has it that it was the tripod for a giant's cooking cauldron.

TOWARDS ARDMINISH
Isle of Gigha

"Out of the world and into Gigha" goes a saying still heard in the west sometimes, and this small island off the coast of Kintyre feels different even by Hebridean standards. Yet it is one of the most accessible of the islands; thousands flock here every year to enjoy the famous Achamore Gardens at Gigha's southern end. The botanical extravaganza contrived here highlights the peculiar advantages of the Hebridean climate: the warm waters of the Gulf Stream ensure that it never gets really cold.

TOWARDS THE CUILLINS
Gesto Bay, Isle of Skye

"Rising on the other side of sorrow", in the stirring words of
Skye's most famous modern Gaelic poet, Sorley Maclean, the
Cuillin Hills form a dramatic backdrop to this view of Skye.
Literally, in this case, they rise on the other side of Loch
Harport, as much a challenge to climbers as an inspiration to
poets. Gaelic tradition holds that the Cuillins were named
after the Irish hero Cuchulain, but scholars suggest a less
colourful etymology – from 'Kjöllen', an Old Norse word
meaning 'keel-shaped ridges'.

DUART CASTLE
Torosay, Isle of Mull

A useful corrective to the view that the Scottish climate is
uniformly cold and wet: here Highland cattle paddle in the sea
to escape the heat of a summer afternoon. Across the bay in the
distance can be seen the distinctive outline of Duart Castle. It
was built in the thirteenth century but was pretty much ruined
by the eighteenth. Since 1910, however, an ambitious restoration
programme undertaken by successive Maclean chiefs has
ensured that Duart is one of the very finest Scottish castles.

TOBERMORY HARBOUR
Isle of Mull

"Tobermorie is an excellent harbour," enthused James Boswell in
1773. Even his companion Dr Johnson conceded that it was "a
busy place". Praise indeed from the sage who said that "the man
who is tired of London is tired of life". The metropolis of Mull is
somewhat smaller than the capital of England, it must be admitted:
even today its population only just tops the 800 mark. As this
scene shows, however, Tobermory is a place to be reckoned with: a
handsome settlement in a truly magnificent setting.

PORTNAHAVEN
Isle of Islay

"Very good for fishing, inhabited and manured" noted Dean Monro approvingly on his visit to this Islay village in 1549. Portnahaven has grown little in the centuries since, but it still presents an impression of prosaic industry and orderliness that even a romantic island sunset cannot set aside. The local fishery has declined; instead, Portnahaven has become the centre for a new industry that could grow inestimably in importance in the years to come: the wave-powered generation of electricity.

DUNVEGAN CASTLE
Isle of Skye

The chiefs of the Clan Macleod have made their homes here since the twelfth century, though much of the present structure dates from the sixteenth. It was a perfect situation: Dunvegan Loch offered a superbly sheltered anchorage – for a long time, indeed, the castle could only be entered from the sea. The 'fairy flag' kept here is said to have been given to a Macleod by his fairy lover many centuries since. It was to be waved in the time of the clan's direst adversity when it would summon supernatural assistance.

KILNAVE CHAPEL AND CROSS
Loch Gruinart, Isle of Islay

A badly damaged Celtic cross stands beside the ruined chapel at Kilnave, while the grey waters of Loch Gruinart lap the shore nearby. All in all, a fittingly desolate scene for a hideous crime, committed four centuries ago in the vicious clan warfare of 1598. A group of fleeing MacLeans, it is said, took refuge here from the MacDonalds. Unimpressed by the fact that their foes had sought sanctuary in a hallowed place, their pursuers simply set the chapel on fire and burned them alive.

DISTILLERY
Lagavulin, Isle of Islay

Scotch whisky is famous the world over: there are scores of single malts on sale, but for many conoisseurs the finest come from Islay. There are fashions in these things, and recently it seems that the Islay malts are in vogue to the extent that Lagavulin whisky has had to be rationed. The distilleries at Ardbeg, Bowmore, Caol Ila and Port Ellen are doing just as well. The secret lies in the 'peaty' quality of these whiskies: the malt for them is smoked over peat-burning fires.

ROTHESAY HARBOUR
Isle of Bute

Rothesay has been a haven for coastal shipping for at least a thousand years. It was officially declared a 'royal burgh' in 1401. This was historically significant in ensuring that Bute stayed firmly in the Scottish sphere of influence, rather than in that of the Lordship of the Isles. The bustling harbour, long a landing-place for fish, is now a popular port of call for pleasure craft – so much so that Rothesay has (quite unfairly) gained a reputation as a tourist trap.

TOWARDS BEN MORE
Loch na Keal, Isle of Mull

Looking southward across the loch, the mass of Ben More
dominates the skyline: at 966 m (3,169 ft) it is Mull's highest
mountain. It is, indeed, the feature for which the island as a
whole was originally named: the Gaelic word 'Mull' translates as
'mass of hill'. The western coast of the island is especially
attractive. Rare orchids, irises and other plant species grow here
in abundance, colonies of nesting guillemots crowd its cliffs and
its hidden inlets are a haven for families of seals.

PIPER
Easdale, Seil

A local piper takes a breather in between performances for
visitors – this island group is now largely dedicated to the tourist
trade. But Easdale grew to prosperity on the back of its fine
black slate, extracted from coastal quarries between the tides.
Production began in the sixteenth century, and business boomed
through Victorian times, by which point gigantic steam-powered
pumps were enabling digging to take place below sea-level. After
1900, however, the industry went into decline as concrete and
ceramic tiles began to take the place of slates.

GYLEN CASTLE
Isle of Kerrera

The MacDougalls built this impressive castle in 1582, but it
was burnt down by Sir James Leslie's Covenanters in 1642.
So called because, in 1638, they had signed a 'National
Covenant' refusing to compromise their Presbyterian beliefs
and practices as England's King Charles I had demanded, the
Covenanters fought bravely for religious freedom. The
English king's interference had been resented both on
nationalistic and religious grounds: soon, of course, his own
country's puritans would tire of his high church sympathies
and dictatorial ways.

TOWARDS THE CUILLINS
Gauskavaig Bay, Isle of Skye

Looking out from the northern shore of the Sleat Peninsula, this panoramic prospect across Gauskavaig Bay and Loch Eishort is dominated by the distant forms of the snowy Cuillins. Closer to hand, however, at the end of the rocky headland to the right of the picture, may be seen the massive stack on which Dunsgaith Castle squats. This was the home of the MacDonalds until the sixteenth century and, though little of the ruin actually remains, the natural fortifications are formidable enough.

KILORAN BAY
Isle of Colonsay

Atlantic rollers pound the sand of this most beautiful of sandy beaches. The tropic blue of the sea should not be too surprising. The Gulf Stream washes the Hebrides, and if it carries with it abundant moisture to fall as rain, it also brings balmy warmth to this improbable riviera of the north. It brings other things too, notably nickernut seed pods fallen from trees in the Caribbean and borne here by the current. These were once worn as good-luck charms by the islanders, who sensed their exoticism.

GRAMPIANS AND ABERDEEN

It is extraordinary how attitudes and understandings change: "To the southern inhabitants of Scotland", wrote Dr Johnson in the 1770s, "the state of the mountains and the islands is equally unknown with that of Borneo and Sumatra."

To the English, of course, these lands seemed still more remote – and with none of the enticing exoticism Johnson's comparison suggests. To them the Highlands were a wasteland; quite literally a waste of land. With the nineteenth century, however, came a shift in sensibility. In the age of Romanticism, bleak was beautiful, and the more wild and rugged the scenery the better. The poems and novels of Sir Walter Scott at once responded to and helped mould this change of taste. The fashion found an influential patron in Her Majesty, Queen Victoria, who had her own castle built at Balmoral, on what now became 'Royal Deeside'.

The royal connection continues, and still draws many thousands of sightseers to the region each year, though people also come to walk, climb, bike and birdwatch – and simply to enjoy the rugged grandeur of the Grampians. In fact, there is no sign whatsoever of the mountains going out of fashion: new visitors are discovering its beauties every year.

CRATHIE KIRK
Balmoral, Grampian

Seen here across a field of rape, Crathie Kirk is the Queen's parish church, where the royal family worships when in residence at Balmoral. The old kirk being deemed inadequate to its new place in the public eye, the present structure was built in 1895, though it is still fitted out very plainly in the Church of Scotland style. There are memorials here to many departed members of the royal family, whilst a monument in the churchyard commemorates Queen Victoria's friend and trusted servant John Brown.

BUCHNESS LIGHTHOUSE
Boddam, Aberdeenshire

Standing at Boddam, the Buchan Ness was built in 1827. It was designed by Robert Stevenson, grandfather of the famous novelist (who would eventually help him edit his memoir of an engineering life). Equipped with a flashing light, the first in Scotland, the new light was crucial given the mounting significance of the fishing port of Peterhead to the north. There was also a growing traffic of vessels to and from Boddam itself, including heavy carriers for the pink granite for which the area was becoming famed.

STONEHAVEN HARBOUR
Aberdeenshire

"Stonehive" wrote one eighteenth-century traveller, was "a little fishing town, remarkable for nothing but its harbour." Today that judgement seems a little harsh. But, as night falls on the British fishing industry, and North Sea oil production too appears to have passed its zenith, communities all along Scotland's eastern coast are facing challenges. There are good grounds for hope, however: these towns have weathered many a storm in the past, and there is every reason to suppose that they will weather many more.

DUNNOTTAR CASTLE
Stonehaven, Aberdeenshire

The morning mist adds a hint of mystery to this prospect of Dunnottar Castle, an impressive ruin south of Stonehaven in the heart of the coastal strip known as 'the Mearns'. The Gaelic name Dunnottar means 'the castle on the point' and that description still largely sums up the place today. Irish sources state that there was a fort here from about AD 680; it is known to have been besieged by Vikings in the AD 890s, but the present structure dates from the twelfth to fifteenth centuries.

BALLINDALLOCH CASTLE
Banffshire

Ballindalloch is one of Scotland's castles that is picturesque at
any time of year, but is particularly so when spring arrives.
Inevitably, it has been restored and altered a good deal since
first constructed. In particular, extensive renovations had to be
made after the damage done by the Marquis of Montrose in
1645. As controversial a figure as he was colourful, Montrose
had first embraced the Covenanters' cause then gone over to
the Government, for whom he proved a brilliant general.
The destruction of Ballindalloch was just one of his triumphs

TORMORE DISTILLERY
Speyside, Grampian

Just over a mile west of Ballindalloch, Strathspey, the
Tormore distillery was established in 1958 – the first new
distillery to be built in the Highlands for sixty years. A risky
step, perhaps, but it turned out to have been a triumph:
Tormore has been one of the most sought-after malts in recent
years. Sir Albert Richardson designed the distillery in a spirit
of elegance and fun. The grounds boast ornamental fountains
and a lake, while the main building has attractive dormer
windows and a tiny belfry.

SLAINS CASTLE
Cruden, Aberdeenshire

Much (and ineptly) modified since its first construction in the early seventeenth century, Slains is neither the most attractive nor the most authentic of Scotland's castles. But you would have to go a long way to find one that was more atmospheric than this gaunt ruin that seems to teeter atop a giddy cliff just north of Cruden, Aberdeenshire. Bram Stoker was inspired by Slains to write his story of *Dracula* (1897), which features "a vast ruined castle, from whose windows came no ray of light".

CROVIE
Banffshire

Houses cling to the coastline in the little village of Crovie, Banffshire, jostling for space between shingle shore and precipitous cliffs. The scourge of so many other British towns and villages, motor traffic does not even get a look-in here, so steep and winding is the only access road. Crovie is thus more isolated than many apparently much remoter places. It has its inconveniences, but perfectly suits those holidaymakers who feel the extra effort is a price worth paying in return for such a quiet retreat.

GOURDON
Aberdeenshire

This small Aberdeenshire fishing village still thrives in its quiet way while larger ports along the coast have been badly damaged by decline. Fish are landed here regularly, and there are several smokeries. The natural harbour here is believed to have been used by Neolithic fishermen 5,000 years ago: a prehistoric burial mound is to be seen outside the village. Gourdon's 'Old Harbour' is very new in comparison: it was built by Thomas Telford in 1819. A second harbour was added forty years later.

BRIG O'DEE
Braemar, Grampian

The old Brig o'Dee, outside Braemar, was built by military engineers in the eighteenth century, when the Hanoverians were desperate to suppress the Jacobite spirit once and for all. Queen Victoria was as aware as anyone of the irony that this sometime hotbed of sedition should have been reinvented in her reign as 'Royal Deeside'. She loved the romance of Jacobitism, in fact, like just about everybody else at the time, even if she never took its claims to a Stewart succession seriously.

TOWARDS LOSSIEMOUTH
Morayshire

Lossiemouth stands, appropriately enough, at the mouth of the River Lossie. The splendid sands around it have been a crucial factor in its development. The inland burgh of Elgin once had its own small port at Spynie, a couple of miles upriver, but drifting sand and silt effectively blocked off its access to the sea. Hence, in the eighteenth century, the establishment of Lossiemouth, right on the very edge of the Moray Firth. In the twentieth century it took on a new role as an appealing holiday resort.

CRAIGIEVAR CASTLE
Alford, Aberdeenshire

This famous pile outside Alford, Aberdeenshire, was
built more for show than for military substance if the
truth be told. Its original owner, William Forbes, was a merchant
in the Baltic trade, and he had the castle built in 1610–18. Its
magnificence can hardly be disputed, though, and it has been
beautifully looked after since being built, with the result that
many of its original Jacobean fittings still remain. It is now in
the care of the National Trust for Scotland.

BALMORAL CASTLE
Grampian

"This dear paradise" was how Queen Victoria described her
favourite part of the world, and there is no more heavenly time
of year on Royal Deeside than the spring. She had Balmoral
Castle built in 1853–5, and it was designed by her beloved
Prince Consort Albert, with the assistance of architect William
Smith. Generations of royals since have come to love the peace
and seclusion they have been able to find on the Balmoral estate
and the uplifting magnificence of the surrounding countryside.

KING'S COLLEGE
Aberdeen

The founding institution of the modern university, King's College was established in 1495, although the fine crown tower was not built until the following century. By that time Aberdeen itself was already a long-established burgh. 'New Aberdeen' had been chartered in 1153. No city named 'Aberdeen' had actually existed before that date, in fact: the old town seems to have been known as 'Aberdon'. As that Gaelic name implies, it was situated to the mouth of the River Don. The district of Old Aberdeen retains a distinctive character.

ROYAL NAVY SHIP
Aberdeen Harbour

"Aberdeen", wrote John Hardyng in 1415, had "a goodly port and haven" – here it is occupied by a vessel of the Royal Navy. In the 1720s, novelist Daniel Defoe described the Aberdonians as "universal merchants trading to Holland, France, Hamburg, Norway, Gothenburg and to the Baltic. It was on the basis of this busy commerce that the 'Granite City' grew. It remains handsome, despite the best efforts of the 1960s planners, and setbacks for a North Sea oil industry that, for a while, made this a boom-town.

CENTRAL SCOTLAND

All the romance – and many of the contradictions – of Scotland is summed up in the figure of 'Rob Roy' MacGregor. A real person, he was born near Loch Katrine in 1671, but he was also a fictional character – most famously in Sir Walter Scott's novel of 1818, though his legend was well-established by that time.

If Rob Roy's historical status is ambiguous, so too was his moral nature, as he lived both within and outside the law. The true-life MacGregor (who, typically, confused things by calling himself 'Campbell' in honour of his mother) was the quite legitimate owner of extensive lands to the east of Loch Lomond. Yet he was simultaneously a brigand, raiding Lowland farms with his men and stealing cattle, or extorting money in a form of protection rackets. He was not officially outlawed until after the Jacobite rebellion of 1715, in which he had (apparently reluctantly) participated in the Stewart cause.

An unlikely icon? Not in English eyes, in which Scotland is still at once stirringly wild but fundamentally friendly; nor in the context of a Scotland that even today has mixed feelings about the Union. It is hard to resist reading that ambivalence into the landscape of Central Scotland: romantic, un-English, but essentially beautiful and benign.

AUTUMN COLOURS
Kenmore, Perthshire

"The village of Kenmore, with its neat church and cleanly houses, stands on a gentle eminence at the end of the water." Dorothy Wordsworth visited Loch Tay with her poet brother in 1803. Thanks to the care of successive Earls of Breadalbane, very little here has actually changed since then, though the cycle of the seasons has meant that no day has been quite the same. Here the colours of autumn give a wonderful warmth and richness to the view, but Kenmore is lovely at any time of year.

ROBERT THE BRUCE STATUE
Bannockburn, Stirling

The mounted figure of Robert I, 'The Bruce', dominates the field at Bannockburn, outside Stirling, just as it did on that fateful day in 1314. On that day, the Scottish King led from the front, guiding his force to an historic victory over the much larger army of England's Edward II. Comparable triumphs would be in short supply over the centuries that followed. Despite this – and despite the Union of 1707 – patriotic fervour still runs high, and Scots of every political hue take pride in the achievement of Bannockburn.

HIKER
Loch Tulla, Perthshire

There is more to a landscape than land: air and water are
essential elements that help give the Scottish scenery its
unique appeal. The spreading sky, the sparkling lochs that
seem to lie around every bend in the road – without these
the mountains might be drear indeed. Here a Highland hiker
pauses to enjoy the sight of Loch Tulla and its magnificent
setting, just to the north of Bridge of Orchy, on the road to
Rannoch and Glencoe.

STIRLING CASTLE
Stirling

Striveling, 'place of strife', seems to have been Stirling's original
Anglo-Saxon name, and it could hardly have been more
appropriate for a fortress-town which controlled the main route
to the north. William Wallace defeated the English at Stirling
Bridge in 1297, taking the castle for the Scots; the field of
Bannockburn is just a few miles away. The castle was fought over
again in the seventeenth century when General Monck captured
it for Cromwell, and again in the eighteenth, when Bonnie
Prince Charlie tried, but failed, to take it.

BIRCH TREES
Aberfeldy, Perthshire

"Come, let us spend the lightsome days / In the birks of Aberfeldie!" Robert Burns' amorous invitation put Aberfeldy on the tourist map 200 years ago, and Dorothy Wordsworth was just one of a throng of eager visitors roaming up and down the valley, attempting to identify which particular *birks* (birch trees) Scotland's national bard had had in mind. There is really no way of knowing, but local tradition proposes this beauty spot by the River Tay: it is indeed a wonderfully romantic setting.

DRUMMOND CASTLE GARDENS
Crieff, Perthshire

Dating from the fifteenth century, Drummond Castle, outside Crieff, is handsome enough, but it is comprehensively upstaged by its spectacular gardens. These were laid out in the seventeenth century in the extravagant Baroque style of the day, the designers paying particular attention to French and Italian models. This is hyper-horticulture, the garden at its farthest imaginable remove from nature. The total effect is magnificent, even mesmerizing, yet profoundly 'un-Scottish' too, it might be felt, by those for whom a certain romantic wildness is the vital key to Caledonian beauty.

PANORAMA
Dundee

"Jute, Jam and Journalism" were famously the formula for
Dundee's prosperity, though the city had first come to
prominence as centre for the whaling industry. None of these
trades was destined to survive the twentieth century intact,
though a downsized D.C. 'Beano' Thomson still has a presence.
Of more significance now is the university, whose tower by
the Tay can be seen here. Along with a major teaching hospital
and a science park on the outskirts, this is enabling the city to
move forward into a high-tech future.

EBRADOUR DISTILLERY
Pitlochry, Perthshire

Scotland's smallest and most picturesque distillery, Ebradour
represents living whisky history, still using a 'worm' that was
constructed in 1825. A coiled copper pipe, cooled in a tub of
water, the worm was in most places superseded by more
efficient condensers of modern design. More efficient maybe,
but less characterful, say critics, who claim the difference is
discernible in the finished product. Those few distilleries which
kept to the old ways have seen business boom in recent years,
whilst at least one modernizer has moved to reinstate the worm.

KILLIN
Perthshire

A wonderful winter view across to the village of Killin, near the head of Loch Tay, with the old bridge across the Falls of Dochart in the foreground. The eighteenth century saw a miniature industrial revolution along these rapids, their energy being harnessed by a series of water mills. These became the basis for a fast-growing textile trade: linen was manufactured here from local flax. Today water from Loch Tay is used to drive turbines producing hydroelectric power, but the Falls of Dochart themselves have been left unspoiled.

REDCASTLE

Angus

Scotland's popularity is paradoxical: tourists have struggled to reach the least accessible reaches of the Highlands and Islands, but the East Coast has been comparatively neglected. A busy commercial corridor for many centuries, this region still has superb travel links today. Much of its coastline, though, remains miraculously unspoiled; if the views are softer, less rugged than the West's, they can be every bit as delightful. Here we look across the dunes from Lunan Water to the village of Redcastle, in Angus.

THE LAKE OF MENTEITH

Stirling

Definitely a 'lake' rather than a 'loch', this is the only stretch of water so-called in Scotland. Scholars suggest that this anomaly may result from confusion over the use of the Gaelic word *laigh* meaning 'low ground'. But by any name, this is a spellbinding place, especially when, as here, a silent dawn tinges the sky above the Trossachs. On an island in the lake stand the ruins of the old Augustinian priory of Inchmahome, founded by Walter Comyn in 1238.

HUNTING TOWER
Kinnoull Hill, Perthshire

A little glimpse of the Rhineland in the Tay Valley, Kinnoull
Tower perches atop a rugged outcrop a few miles east of Perth,
the stone-built souvenir of an aristocrat's continental holiday.
A folly it may be, but it is a glorious one: it dominates the
landscape for miles up and down the valley. And its conception
was not entirely whimsical. The ninth Earl of Kinnoull, who
had the tower built in the eighteenth century, seems to have
seen it as a job-creation scheme in a difficult economic time.

LOCH LOMOND
Dumbartonshire

Britain's largest freshwater lake is also, in the opinion of many, its
most beautiful, a haven for those who love messing about in boats.
In the past its waters have been a busy thoroughfare – the remains
of dugout canoes have been found, along with the clinker-built,
stern-steered *birlinn* galleys of Gaelic times. But it was with the
coming of the steamship that Loch Lomond really came into its
own. Trips on the loch departed regularly from the pier at Balloch,
a favourite day-trip for generations of Glaswegian children.

TOWARDS LOCH RANNOCH AND SCHIEHALLION
Perthshire

One of Scotland's most distinctive mountains is seen here reflected in the waters of Loch Rannoch to entrancing effect, but there has always been an air of enchantment about Schiehallion. The Gaelic name, *Sìdh Chaillean*, means 'Fairy Hill of the Caledonians', and few visitors are able to resist its magic. It is ironic, in the circumstances, that scientists Nevil Maskelyne and John Playfair should in 1774 have used the slopes of Schiehallion for the least mystical of purposes: that of estimating the mass of planet Earth.

GLAMIS CASTLE
Angus

Glamis was, of course, one of the thanages of Shakespeare's Macbeth: he really existed, though the historical details are hopelessly obscure. King Malcolm II of Scotland is said to have been murdered here in 1034, and his grandson Duncan at Cawdor six years later. We are on much safer ground with more recent royals: this was the childhood home of the late Queen Mother, and the birthplace of the late Princess Margaret. The present Glamis Castle was built in the early fifteenth century but radically remodelled 200 years later.

EDINBURGH, LOTHIAN AND FIFE

Today Edinburgh is famous the world over for its festivals. Every aspect of the arts and media is celebrated here. Though the top performers in music, theatre and other artistic fields flock each year to the official International Festival, the so-called 'Fringe Festival' has in some ways surpassed it in significance.

Add to this important film and TV events, plus the world's most successful International Book Festival and it becomes clear why the Edinburgh 'brand' is acknowledged everywhere.

But then Scotland has always been an outward-looking country, with the Scots seeing themselves as citizens of a wider world. At times this has been a matter of strategy: from Mary, Queen of Scots to Bonnie Prince Charlie, Scots leaders have hoped that contacts 'across the water' would help them outflank England.

There is much more to it than anti-Englishness, though. The old kingdom of Scotland was very much a maritime nation, its trade with the Baltic a key to its prosperity. From Leith, Dunfermline and a host of now-forgotten ports in Fife and the Firth of Forth, close relations with the Continent were maintained. Today that traffic has declined, but the cultural commerce has continued: this region has become Scotland's window on the world.

TOWARDS EDINBURGH CASTLE
Princes Street Gardens, Edinburgh

The ancient British writer Gildas, writing 1,500 years ago, tells us that the Celtic Goddodin tribe had a hilltop fort at 'Etyn'. The castle on its rocky outcrop dominates Edinburgh to this day. For centuries, however, it would not have been seen from this exact angle, as the present-day Princes Street Gardens were originally under water. Not until 1763 was the Nor' Loch drained, clearing the way for the construction of a more spacious and elegant New Town, of which Princes Street itself would mark the southern edge.

POPPIES
Dunbar, East Lothian

Daisies jostle with poppies in a colourful crowd, setting the whole landscape shimmering in this field outside Dunbar, East Lothian. The countryside in this part of Scotland is generally far softer and gentler than it is in the wilds of the west and north. Yet as the hill at the horizon reminds us, the Lowlands are by no means uniformly level – or even 'low'. While the spectacular summits of the Highlands are absent, there is considerable scenic variety, including areas of hilly terrain.

THORNTONLOCH
Torness, East Lothian

Its sandstone set ablaze by the rays of an evening sun, a rocky arch is reflected in a pool at Thorntonloch, East Lothian. Just a few miles away, thousands thunder past each day on the A1 and on the main East Coast railway line, but this beautiful coast stays one of Scotland's best-kept secrets. There are superb bathing beaches, wonderful walks and some of Britain's best birdwatching to be had here, while some of Scotland's finest golf courses lie just inland.

TOWARDS LINLITHGOW PALACE
Linlithgow Loch, West Lothian

A winter sun sinks slowly behind the Palace of Linlithgow, viewed across the icy waters of Linlithgow Loch. Mary, Queen of Scots was born here in 1542, and her unhappy story still seems to haunt the place. Her deposition from the throne, her flight into England and her imprisonment and eventual execution there on Elizabeth's orders, would certainly bring bad fortune to Linlithgow. No longer a royal residence, it never really thrived under the Anglo-Scottish Union, and remains today a small West Lothian town.

EDINBURGH CASTLE AND ST CUTHBERTS
Edinburgh

Above the trees can be seen the shapely spire of St Cuthberts, its leafy churchyard a peaceful refuge from the noise and bustle of Princes Street. Beyond rises the mass of the Castle Rock, what remains of an extinct volcano, with the castle buildings clustered round the top. The oldest, St Margaret's Chapel, dates from the eleventh century. Every day except Sunday a gun is fired from the battlements at one o'clock in the afternoon. Originally this was done so ships in Leith Harbour could check their chronometers.

HOPETOUN HOUSE
West Lothian

This was an ordinary West Lothian mansion when it was built for the Hope family at the end of the seventeenth century. By 1730, however, the family had been ennobled. After this, something statelier seemed to be called for, so the new Earl of Hopetoun brought in William Adam, and over several years first he and then his sons John and Robert went to work. They re-created the house along its present, positively palatial lines: it has been described, not altogether fancifully, as a Scottish Versailles.

TANTALLON CASTLE
East Lothian

Dramatically sited on its coastal clifftop, Tantallon Castle was built by the Douglas family around 1375. A curtain wall 12 ft (3.6 m) thick cut this little headland off from the landward side, while safe within rose a round keep six storeys high. The Douglases' regular fallings out with one another and with their kings ensured that the castle saw plenty of action in the fifteenth and sixteenth centuries. In 1651 Cromwell's General Monck subjected it to a twelve-day bombardment, effectively reducing it to ruins.

PRINCES STREET
Edinburgh

Darkness falls on Princes Street, Edinburgh, but it falls on a city that sleeps less and less. The character of the Scottish capital has changed dramatically in recent decades. Once a byword for staidness, it can now boast some of Europe's liveliest nightlife, and young people flock here from all over the world – not just for the Festival but for the vast street celebration now held each year at Hogmanay. Containing three universities and several colleges, the city's tone is more and more being set by the young.

FORTH RAIL BRIDGE
North Queensferry, Fife

This miracle of Victorian engineering, instantly recognizable the world over, celebrated its centenary in 1990. It was designed by John Fowler and Benjamin Baker and built by William Arrol. It joins North Queensferry, Fife (pictured) with South Queensferry on the Lothian side. As their names suggest, a ferry used to ply between these points. The 'queen' concerned was the eleventh-century monarch Margaret, whose son David I ordered monks to establish a service here. A suspension bridge for road traffic was opened in 1964.

TOWARDS CASTLE HILL AND ARTHUR'S SEAT
Edinburgh

Seen from the west, the castle is backed by the crouching form of Arthur's Seat. A half-hearted tradition has it that the legendary king and his knights sleep here awaiting the summons to save Britain in its hour of peril, but English Arthur has never loomed large in a Scottish folk-tradition with any number of home-grown heroes. Arthur's Seat still has magical associations, though: many gather at sunrise on the 1st of May for the Celtic festival of Beltane, climbing to the summit to wash their faces in the dew.

ANSTRUTHER HARBOUR
East Neuk, Fife

Anstruther lies in the picturesque East Neuk of Fife, one of the loveliest – and least known – corners of Scotland. The secret is getting out, though: tourists are coming here in increased numbers, and pleasure craft are beginning to outnumber fishing boats in the harbour. The size of its harbour hints at the importance Anstruther once had, not just for its fishery, but as a port for continental trade. The herring fishery remained crucial, though, and whilst that has declined in recent years, Anstruther is home to the Scottish Fisheries Museum.

ST ANDREW'S CATHEDRAL AND TOWN
Fife

The view from St Rule's Tower, St Andrews shows the edge of
the Cathedral precincts, and the streets of the university city itself.
Prince William, Britain's future king, began studying here in
2001. Although St Andrews' academic excellence and venerable
history were no doubt points in its favour, there can be little
doubt that, for those charged with the Prince's security, the sheer
isolation of this tiny city must have been a recommendation,
situated as it is far out on the northeastern coast of Fife.

PITTENWEEM
East Neuk, Fife

Warmed here on a summer's day, it seems the picture of peace
and repose, but Pittenweem is still a busy fishing centre. It takes
its name from the Gaelic 'Place of the Cave', a reference to St
Fillan's hermitage, just nearby, but in his less reclusive moments
the saint built a successful priory. This became the nucleus of
the modern town. So far it has been strikingly successful in
walking the tightrope between encouraging the tourist trade
and maintaining its own distinctive character as a working port.

KELLIE CASTLE
Pittenweem, Fife

A little way inland from Pittenweem stands Kellie Castle, which was originally built in 1360, but whose present structure largely dates from the sixteenth century. It was always more a home than a fortification, and is now regarded as an important monument to Scottish domestic architecture. Its fine interior fittings from the seventeenth and eighteenth centuries have been lovingly preserved by generations of the Lorimer family, but it is just as appealing without. The largely Jacobean gardens were carefully restored by the castle's current owners, the National Trust for Scotland.

ST ANDREW'S CATHEDRAL
St Andrews, Fife

Looking along what would have been the main aisle of St Andrew's Cathedral from west to east, the visitor cannot help being overwhelmed by its stupendous scale. It seems still more surprising given the tiny size of the city now, and its remoteness from the modern beaten track. In medieval times, however, this was one of the great pilgrimage sites of Europe, on a par with England's Canterbury Cathedral and Santiago de Compostela, Spain. People came from all over Christendom to worship at the Apostle's shrine.

GLASGOW, CLYDE VALLEY AND ARGYLL

Scotland is too often seen in stereotypes. Some, having heard much of its wild beauty, are surprised to find it has any towns at all. Others, brought up on the tough TV cop Taggart, or on the spiky realism of Irvine Welsh's Trainspotting, are more or less unaware of the existence of scenic Scotland.

No region has suffered more from such stereotyping than the west of Scotland, wrongly assumed to be a single, continuous urban sprawl. Granted, Glasgow is the centre of a major modern conurbation, parts of which are not exactly easy on the eye, but there is a great deal more to the region than brick and concrete.

Across much of the region exist scenes of post-industrial dereliction: rusting gantries, abandoned gasholders and dilapidated factories. These, ironically, were once held to represent a heroic future for Scotland; already, it appears, they are monuments to the past. Their failure has meant misery for thousands, but the hope is that new economic opportunities will be found – ones which do not leave such unsightly scars on the Scottish landscape. For, despite the stereotypes, this is still an overwhelmingly lovely part of the world, which must be preserved for future generations.

TOWARDS CASTLE STALKER
Appin, Argyll

Castle Stalker takes centre-stage in this majestic Appin
panorama, with the Morvern Hills behind and the waters
of Loch Laich before. Built in the fifteenth century, the castle
fell into ruins soon after, only to be recommissioned in the
eighteenth century by the Crown. Across Europe, the advent
of the modern era had rendered castles obsolete: even in
Scotland, this had been the case. But, with a series of Jacobite
rebellions making much of the Highlands ungovernable, there
was a clear role for strongholds such as this.

BURIAL CAIRN
Kilmartin, Argyll

As the crow flies, the great city of Glasgow lies less than 40
miles from here, but the roar of urban life never seemed so far
away. And yet, from perhaps 9,000 years ago, there seems to have
been something of a prehistoric metropolis around what is now
the village of Kilmartin in Argyll. Some, like the Nether Largie
Cairns, shown here, are clearly burial sites, but there are also
standing stones and other, unidentified, remains, dating from the
Stone Age through to the Pictish period.

FALLS OF LORA
Loch Etive, Argyll

No ordinary waterfall, the Falls of Lora are in fact a tidal race. Tides fill Loch Etive high, and as they go out, it is left overbrimming. The excess thunders out through the Connel narrows across a rocky shelf. The resulting waves have become a magnet for thrill-seeking canoeists, though only the higher spring tides produce a satisfactory effect. Here, beyond the whitewater, Loch Etive stretches away surprisingly serene, the peak of Ben Cruachan standing out against a distant skyline.

WATERFALL
Glen Kinglas, Argyll

A mountain stream tumbles down Glen Kinglas in one of the most beautiful parts of Argyll, the sight of white water lending its own special exhilaration to the Highland scene. River levels reach their highest with the spring snowmelt and in the wake of the autumn storms, sometimes declining to a trickle in the heat of summer. In the course of the twentieth century, the energy contained in many such torrents was captured and used to drive turbines for the generation of hydroelectric power.

LOCH AWE
Argyll

Looking down on to the Pass of Brander from Ben
Cruachan, rugged crags crowd threateningly in upon the
aptly named Loch Awe. According to Celtic legend, the
Cailleach Bheur, the crone of winter, originated here – as
the goddess Bheithir, she tended a well of youth. One night
she accidentally let its waters drain away, and they collected
below in what is now Loch Awe. In their fury, the other
gods cast her out from their immortal company and she
became the spiteful storm goddess, howling round the
hilltops all winter long.

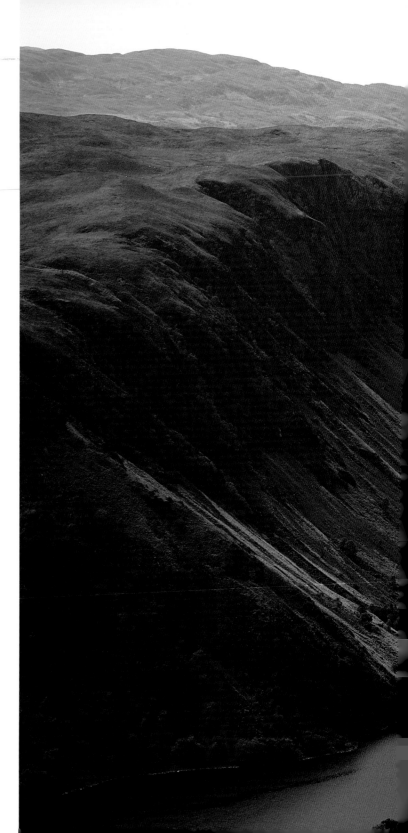

BEN CRUACHAN
Argyll

This is a land for all seasons. Every time of year has its special
quality, and it is impossible to decide which displays the
Scottish scenery to its best advantage. Here, the first touch
of autumn tinges the trees as we look across the River Orchy
to Ben Cruachan, the warmth of the colours dispelling any
chill in the upland air. Just a few miles long, the Orchy flows
into Loch Awe, whose waters in their turn find their way
down the Pass of Brander to Loch Etive.

SUNSET
Oban Bay, Argyll

Oban Bay lies ashimmer beneath a setting sun, the dark outline
of Kerrera beyond. A jewel in its own right, this little island has
the important secondary function of providing a natural
breakwater for Oban. Savage storms lash this coast each year,
tearing up the Firth of Lorne, but Kerrera bears the brunt,
allowing Oban a sheltered anchorage. Further still across the
water can be seen the Isles of Mull (left) and Lismore (right),
with the hills of Morvern just discernible on the far horizon.

DUNSTAFFNAGE BAY
Oban, Argyll

Fishing boats and pleasure craft now share the crowded waters of Dunstaffnage Bay, a sheltered inlet just outside the entrance to Loch Etive. An important anchorage for many centuries, it was protected by a series of strongholds, dating back at least as early as the fifth century. In those days, Argyll formed part of the kingdom of Dál Riada which brought together southwestern Scotland and much of Ulster in a single realm. The present castle was built around the beginning of the thirteenth century.

FIRTH OF LORNE
Argyll

A purple sky stains the mist and the mountains and an eerie stillness reigns as dawn breaks over the Firth of Lorne. Ironically, the name of Connel, the Argyll settlement from where this picture was taken, is thought to have come from the Gaelic *conghail*, a word meaning 'turbulent water'. This is a clear reference to the nearby Falls of Lora, but that is a tidal phenomenon, coming round in regular cycles: on a windless morning like this the water could hardly be calmer here.

LOCH FYNE
Argyll

Winter reflections upon Loch Fyne highlight wispy clouds
and a grey-silk sky endowing Glen Kinglas with a distinctly
ethereal air. At the head of the glen rises Ben Ime, but there is
access to Glen Croe via the famous pass known as 'Rest and
Be Thankful'. That name was inscribed beside a grassy bench
left there by General Wade's engineers who built a road here
in the eighteenth century. The new military roads helped open
up the Highlands economically, though drovers disliked their
narrow tracks and hard metalled surfaces.

CUTTY SARK RACE
Greenock, Renfrewshire

"This grey town", wrote local poet John Davidson, "that pipes the morning up before the lark / With shrieking steam, and from a hundred stalks / Lacquers the sooty sky…" Now the steamship funnels have been replaced by the flag-festooned masts of pleasure yachts (or, in this case, the tall ships of the Cutty Sark race), the skies are blue and Greenock harbour anything but "grey". The rest of the town has a forlorn look, though, now its industrial glory days are gone, but is making the difficult transition to new economic times.

SPRING
Eaglesham, Renfrewshire

Spring comes to rural Renfrewshire in a shower of blossom. Farther up the hillside can be seen what one visitor in 1799 described as "the pleasant village of Eaglesham". It was brand-new, then, of course, built by local landowners the Earls of Eglinton as a centre for handloom-weaving, and the passage of time has only made it seem more "pleasant" still. In 1960 it became the first village in Scotland to be listed as a place of special historic architectural interest, an honour which was thoroughly deserved.

BARCALDINE CASTLE
Benderloch, Argyll

Built in the early years of the sixteenth century, Barcaldine
Castle, Benderloch, is often known as the 'Black Castle',
supposedly on account of the dark colour of its stones.
In this exquisite midwinter scene, however, frost and snow
have enveloped everything in sparkling white, from the grassy
tussocks in the foreground to the hills of Appin on the far
horizon. In the middle distance can just be seen the grey
waters of Loch Creran. Barcaldine commanded the entrance
to this strategically important sea loch.

ARCHWAY
Kilmartin, Argyll

Kilmartin is justly famous for its prehistoric remains: there
are 150 sites in the village and surrounding area. But it has
had a more recent history, too. Bridges had been built over the
Kilmartin Burn by the beginning of the seventeenth century
and road access attained by the middle of the eighteenth.
This thriving settlement created monoliths of its own – the
churchyard (from which this photograph was taken) contains
a marvellous collection of grave slabs dating from the
fourteenth to the eighteenth centuries.

MCCAIG'S TOWER
Oban, Argyll

"The Ramsgate of the Highlands", observed Virginia Woolf
a little waspishly in 1938; "only the Scots having melancholy
in their bones ... being entirely without frivolity build even
bathing sheds of granite let alone hotels. The result is grim."
The famous novelist could not even bring herself, it seems,
to comment on McCaig's Tower, a replica of the Colosseum
built by a local businessman in 1897: perhaps we should all
be grateful for that fact. Happily, many thousands of visitors
have since disagreed profoundly with her assessment.

JAMES WATT
BORN 1736. DIED 1819.

GEORGE SQUARE
Glasgow

James Watt had the inspiration for his steam condenser when he was walking across Glasgow Green in 1764, and it earned him this statue in George Square. Glasgow had been a thriving merchant city and seat of learning for generations before the Industrial Revolution, but engineering was undoubtedly the making of the modern city. Steel, shipbuilding and other heavy industries made this the 'second city of the Empire' for a time, but it has struggled to find an economic identity in the post-industrial age.

RIVER KELVIN
Kelvingrove Park, Glasgow

To walk beside the River Kelvin on an afternoon in summer is quickly to forget the busy city so close at hand. Above the trees beyond the weir appears the spire of the university, which was originally established in 1451. The great Victorian building boom has left us with a false impression of Glasgow, and it is a much more venerable place than is generally assumed. It was founded in the sixth century, and its cathedral dates from the thirteenth: it was old before the first steam-hammer was ever built.

SOUTHWEST SCOTLAND

Scotland's southwestern counties have remained almost entirely unknown to outsiders, despite perhaps being the country's most accessible part. Just across the border from Carlisle the main road northward takes the traveller through a region of lovely, if understated, scenery, with towns and villages as pretty as any in the British Isles.

That is the point, of course: this has always been a region that wayfarers passed through on their way to the cities of the Central Lowlands and beyond. As for Galloway and Ayrshire, lying farther westward, these have to a large extent been by-passed by modern tourism as surely as they were by-passed by so much of modern history. Had it not been for the road (and, until the 1960s, the railway) to Stranraer, and the ferry from there to Ireland, it seems reasonable to wonder whether any outsider would have come this way at all.

Even now, the vagaries of the transmitter system mean many here have to watch Northern Irish television – the southwest is in some ways semi-detached from the rest of Scotland. Yet it is also one of the most beautiful areas of the country, with a fascinating history and a very special character all of its own.

CARLINGWARK LOCH
Castle Douglas, Dumfries and Galloway

A perfectly good little market town stood here just over 200 years ago when local aristocrat William Douglas applied for burgh status for a new town. His family had been based at nearby Threave Castle for generations; unsurprisingly, perhaps, he felt he owned the place. The new settlement, Castle Douglas, was built over the old site, whose name endures only in that of Carlingwark Loch and lies just to the south of the town centre. However high-handed its founder, Castle Douglas is today a very pleasant place.

GATEHOUSE OF FLEET
Kirkcudbrightshire

Gatehouse of Fleet was made – and arguably saved – by paternalism. The town as we see it was built in the eighteenth century, James Murray of Cally planning the whole place, with tannery, textile works and other places of manufacture, all driven by water mills. The nineteenth century saw a slow decline and then with the twentieth came tourism which, seizing on such a delightful spot, seemed set to destroy it. But Mrs Murray Usher, James' descendant, set strict controls on new development, so preserving one of Scotland's most attractive towns.

GREAT CUMBRAE

Ayrshire

A replica vintage van lines up for the ferry from Great
Cumbrae island to Largs, a town which grew to prosperity as
a port of call for pleasure steamers. That trade has largely
declined, but ferries still criss-cross the Firth of Clyde,
maintaining contacts between the Ayrshire coast and a host of
offshore islands. And if the coastal pleasure cruise is becoming
a thing of the past, the ferry is still fun – for children, especially,
it is often the most memorable part of an island holiday!

AILSA CRAIG

Girvan, Ayrshire

The form of Ailsa Craig on the horizon looks like some great
leviathan rising from the waves in this unusual panorama across
the town of Girvan. A huge rock or a tiny island? It is hard to
say, but this granite mass is both bigger and more distant than it
looks, lying some 10 miles (17 km) off the Ayrshire coast and
standing over 340 m (1,100 ft) high. There are the remains of a
castle there, as well as considerable colonies of seabirds,
including puffins, guillemots and gannets.

AYR
Ayrshire

Long a prosperous market town, by the 1780s Ayr was a
significant port, with some 300 vessels calling every year.
Add in the growing tourist trade, helped on by Ayr's association
with that great romantic icon, Robert Burns, and it can be
imagined how heady the mood was here in the nineteenth
cntury. Ayr was, according to Robert Chambers, "a handsome
town in a flourishing condition." Handsome it remains, if not
quite flourishing, but Ayr is a considerable place, with much to
offer the visitor even now.

WELLINGTON SQUARE
Ayr, Ayrshire

The size and splendour of the town courthouse, the County
Buildings, seen here across the spacious flowerbeds of
Wellington Square, announce the extent of Ayr's aspirations
when it was built in 1823. It was constructed as part of a major
remodelling closely based on Edinburgh's acclaimed New Town,
and comparisons with the capital were routine. Ayr became a
place of fashion, even boasting its own school for "young ladies
of quality"; one Victorian visitor described it as "a provincial
capital of considerable social standing".

TOWARDS ARRAN
Prestwick, Ayrshire

An Arran sunset, as seen across the Firth of Clyde from
the front at Prestwick, just north of Ayr. Arran is the
southernmost of the major Scottish isles. It is large enough to
have a significant variety of terrains, dividing roughly between
a 'lowland' south and a 'highland' north, but with local variations
too, within those zones. Arran is as rich in wildlife as it is in
prehistoric monuments and medieval castles; its villages are as
picturesque as its scenery is stunning.

KELBURN CASTLE
Largs, Ayrshire

Standing south of Largs, on the Ayrshire coast, this castle
belongs to the Earls of Glasgow and has been in the same family
for 800 years. In fact, for 500 of those, they were simply the
Boyle family: the first earl was ennobled for his work drafting
the documents for the Act of Union of 1707. A controversial
legacy for some – Robert Burns spoke of the "parcel of rogues"
who had sold out Scotland – but there is no disputing the
nobility of the family home.

BURNS MONUMENT
Alloway, Ayrshire

The single arch of the 'Auld Brig o'Doon', from where this photo was taken, was "the largest I ever saw" according to Daniel Defoe, but this little settlement just south of Ayr would soon have a far greater claim to fame. In 1759, Robert Burns, destined to become Scotland's national bard, was born here into a poor farming family. His monument, seen right, seems over-stately for a natural rebel with radical views (and sometimes wayward morals) – but then there was part of him that always yearned for respectable acceptance.

BRUCE'S STONE
Glentrool, Galloway

Not a prehistoric megalith, this monument was raised in 1929 in commemoration of the Battle of Glentrool. In 1307, the miserably depleted force of the all but defeated Robert the Bruce gained an unexpected triumph over a substantial English army. They employed guerrilla tactics, hiding out in these wooded ravines and then toppling boulders down upon the enemy column. It is appropriate, then, that his memorial takes this form, on the hillside above Loch Trool in what is now part of the Galloway Forest Park.

DUNURE CASTLE
Heads of Ayr, Ayrshire

Mary, Queen of Scots saw this dramatic coastline when she stayed in nearby Dunure Castle in the course of a royal progress of 1563. Just a few years later Gilbert Kennedy, Earl of Cassilis, would prove a far less genial host when he roasted a certain Allan Stewart on a spit. The Commendator of Crossraguel Abbey, Stewart had refused to hand over abbey lands which Kennedy had long coveted for himself. Today the castle is a ruin, almost indistinguishable from the rocks of the coast.

TURNBERRY GOLF COURSE
Turnberry, Ayrshire

The 'Maidens of Turnberry', on the Carrick coast a few miles south of Ayr, have created both a haven and a hazard for seaborne craft. A line of rocks, partially-submerged, they comprise a natural harbour, but can be traps too for the unwary navigator. The lighthouse on nearby Turnberry Point was built in the 1870s. Superb even by Scottish standards, the world famous golf-courses just inland were opened in the early twentieth century. The British Open has been held here several times.

BARGANY HOUSE
Dailly, Ayrshire

Azaleas and rhododendrons crowd the banks of a delightful lily pond – just the centrepiece of the splendid Bargany gardens. Bargany House, a few miles north of Girvan, Ayrshire, has been the home of the Dalrymple Hamilton family for centuries. It is beautiful in its own right, but it is the gardens which are its claim to fame, their winding walks and rockeries a veritable blaze of colour. Scottish gardens have a special intensity, it is said, with so much living energy crammed into such a short growing season.

CAERLAVEROCK CASTLE
Solway Firth, Dumfries-shire

The visitor's first impression of Caerlaverock Castle is that half of it must have been razed by the forces of Edward I who besieged it in 1300, or blown up by the Covenanters who captured it in 1640. Only then does it sink in that the present structure, dating from 1425, though a ruin, is remarkably well-preserved but built to a highly unorthodox triangular design. It still cuts an impressive figure on its site above the salt marshes of the Solway Firth.

GIRVAN HARBOUR
Ayrshire

Today Girvan is a busy fishing harbour, with cruises to Ailsa Craig, but its seafarers were not always so innocently employed. Duncan Forbes complained in 1747 that one could hardly find any fish in Scottish markets, so wholeheartedly had the fishing fleet thrown itself into the more lucrative 'runners' trade. There have been times in Scotland's history when smuggling has seemed less a crime than a national duty: a great deal of untaxed tobacco and brandy has been brought in along the Ayrshire coast over the years.

BORDERS

The 'Debatable Land', strictly speaking, lay to the west of the present Borders region, the area lying between the Rivers Esk and Sark. This area was claimed by both Scotland and England for several centuries before it was finally divided up in 1552. But this controversial scrap of land is often taken as emblematic of the Borders as a whole, its character formed in uncertainty and violence.

This was a wild frontier and the culture of the Border reivers really existed, even if its romance may have been concocted by later balladeers and writers. Although tradition may have exaggerated the heroism of their activities, tending to characterize them as 'raids', it has also given a misleading sense of their true scale. Low-level raiding was indeed a way of life on both sides of the border, the English often raiding English neighbours and the Scots attacking their fellow Scots. As well as countless minor forays back and forth, there were also large-scale expeditions, some Scottish campaigns reaching as far south as York.

Fiercely fought over for hundreds of years, this was a country whose ownership may have been up for grabs, but whose sense of Scottishness was only strengthened by that fact.

COUNTRYSIDE
Kelso, Roxburghshire

The rolling country around Kelso could hardly be more peaceful now, but invaders trampled these green fields in days gone by. The Earl of Hertford's men slaughtered the monks of the nearby abbey in 1545, just one entry in a catalogue of killing. The accession of James VI of Scotland to the English throne as James I in 1603 drew the sting from an enmity which was officially abolished with the Act of Union of 1707. But the rivalries – and sometimes the resentments – linger on.

MELLERSTAIN HOUSE
Berwickshire

A few miles to the northwest of Kelso stands the magnificent Mellerstain House, the ancestral seat of the Earls of Haddington. This stupendous pile was begun by the famous Kirkcaldy architect William Adam around 1725 and was completed in the 1770s by his son Robert. Its interior is as impressive as its splendidly landscaped grounds and ornamental gardens, with much of the original paintwork and stucco still surviving. The terrace, with its beautiful balustrade, is a relatively recent addition – it was built by Sir Reginald Blomfield in 1909.

BORDER COUNTRYSIDE
Melrose, Roxburghshire

"I can stand on the Eildon Hills and point out forty-two places famous in war and verse", Sir Walter Scott liked to say. Most modern visitors will be content just to enjoy the scenery. But there is no doubt that the sense of struggles past gives the Border country a unique atmosphere; the spirit of the reivers seems to resonate still. Here we look out from the foot of the Eildons across a now peaceful scene to where the Black Hill rises in the distance.

RIVER TWEED
Ladykirk, Berwickshire

Beyond the river lies England: the frontier follows the meandering course of the lower Tweed before striking off southward into the Cheviot Hills a few miles west of here. Before the bridge was built at Berwick at the end of the thirteenth century, two fords near here were the only easy way across the river and, for several hundred hectic years in the Middle Ages, invasion forces practically commuted back and forth across these shallows. The bridge here was not built until 1901.

SUSPENSION BRIDGE
Peebles, Peebleshire

A suspension bridge spans the River Tweed at Peebles, one of the prettiest towns in the Borders, historically a textiles town but now most famous for its Hydro. This luxury hotel opened in 1881, and its effect was to make the town a genteel and prosperous inland resort, visitors flocking here for fresh air, fishing, bathing and walking, and for touring farther afield through the Border region. The formula was to prove a winning one: the Hydro has continued to thrive, its bookings boosted by a growing conference trade.

SIR WALTER SCOTT'S TOMB
Dryburgh Abbey, Roxburghshire

Amid the ruins of this twelfth-century abbey lie the mortal remains of Sir Walter Scott, for better or worse the inventor of Shortbread Scotland. His impact in works like *Marmion* (1808), *Waverley* (1814) and *The Heart of Midlothian* (1818) can scarcely be overestimated: his stirring stories created Caledoniamania not just in Britain but beyond. Easy as it is to sneer – and his Scotland does seem terribly sentimentalized now – he put the country on the imaginative map for readers around the world.

KELSO ABBEY
Kelso, Roxburghshire

Kelso's monastic community survived the destruction of
the Abbey buildings in 1545, essentially camping out in
appropriated churches and other buildings. With the
Reformation, however, it was suppressed once and for all.
The impact on Kelso was considerable – a medieval monastery
is not just a spiritual centre but an economic hub – but it
managed to make its way as market town. As time went on,
its inhabitants built successful brewing and linen-bleaching
trades; now of course it has a thriving tourist trade.

TEA HOUSE
Mellerstain, Berwickshire

Scotland has many glorious gardens but its weather may not match up, so a summerhouse has to be ready for anything. This tea house is one solution: half baronial castle and half thatched cottage, it stands in the grounds of Mellerstain, home to the Earls of Haddington for generations. Imposing as it is, it strikes an unexpectedly homely note amidst the elaborately formal ornamental gardens of one of Scotland's most palatial Georgian mansions. Perhaps it was deliberately designed as a place of relaxing refuge?

THE EILDON HILLS
Roxburghshire

The Eildon Hills have always been a place of mystery and magic. Here, Thomas of Earlcedoune (Earlston) was supposedly seduced by the Fairy Queen in the thirteenth century. She took him with her into the earth, and he did not emerge for seven years. When he did so, 'Thomas the Rhymer' had the gift of prophecy, foretelling, amongst other things, the Battle of Bannockburn. He became known as 'True Thomas' because he was unable to tell a lie; the folk tradition does not operate under any such restriction.

ST ABBS
Berwickshire

The clifftop walks along the coast around St Abbs are some
of the loveliest in the country – though in a brisk east wind
it can be a rather bracing experience! Full of hidden creeks
and inlets, its rocks are a navigational nightmare for outsiders;
this coast was a centre for smuggling in the eighteenth
century. It was not just the obvious luxuries that were
imported illicitly: wool and hides were both brought in from
the Continent as contraband to escape protectionist tariffs
levied by the Crown.

INDEX